Provinces and Territories of Canada

NOVA SCOTIA

— *"Canada's Ocean Playground"* —

Published by Weigl Educational Publishers Limited
6325 10 Street SE
Calgary, Alberta
T2H 2Z9

www.weigl.com

Library and Archives Canada Cataloguing in Publication data available upon request.
Fax 403-233-7769 for the attention of the Publishing Records department.

ISBN 978-1-55388-978-6 (hard cover)
ISBN 978-1-55388-991-5 (soft cover)

Printed in the United States of America
1 2 3 4 5 6 7 8 9 0   13 12 11 10 09

Editor: Heather C. Hudak
Design: Terry Paulhus

Every reasonable effort has been made to trace ownership and to obtain permission to reprint copyright material. The publishers would be pl‹
to have any errors or omissions brought to their attention so that they may be corrected in subsequent printings.

Weigl acknowledges Getty Images as one of its image suppliers for this title.
Art Gallery of Nova Scotia – Collection of Robert and Betty Flinn, Halifax, Nova Scotia: page 39 middle; Art Gallery of Ontario: page 29; Cana
Tourism Commission: page 42 bottom; Library and Archives Canada: pages 24 bottom, 26 top, 34 bottom; National Gallery of Canada, Ottaᵥ
page 24 top; Rogers Communications Inc: pages 27, 30 top; Royal Ontario Museum: page 31 bottom.

All of the Internet URLs given in the book were valid at the time of publication. However, due to the dynamic nature of the Internet, some ad
may have changed, or sites may have ceased to exist since publication. While the author and publisher regret any inconvenience this may cau
readers, no responsibility for any such changes can be accepted by either the author or the publisher.

We gratefully acknowledge the financial support of the Government of Canada through the Book Publishing Industry Development Program
(BPIDP) for our publishing activities.

Contents

Nova Scotia

Nova Scotia is Latin for "New Scotland." The province was named by a Scottish nobleman who saw its distinct similarity to his homeland. Cape Breton's highland landscape looks very much like the highlands of Scotland. Highlands, along with lush forests, wide fields, sparkling lakes, rushing rivers, and rugged coastlines, all contribute to Nova Scotia's picture-perfect scenery. Nova Scotia's culture is as rich as its scenery. Scottish heritage is evident throughout the province. Mi'kmaq, Acadian, and German communities are also present. Each of these communities adds to the province's diverse identity and festive atmosphere.

Nova Scotia has an area of 55,490 square kilometres. It has about 7,400 km of coastline.

Lunenburg is home to a strong German community.

Nova Scotia is the second-smallest province in Canada. It lies on the east coast, and nowhere in the province is more than an hour's drive to the sea. Nova Scotia, New Brunswick, and Prince Edward Island are Canada's **Maritime Provinces**. Nova Scotia is a **peninsula**. The province is almost entirely surrounded by water. Only a narrow strip of land joins Nova Scotia to the rest of mainland Canada. This strip of land is called the Chignecto Isthmus, and it links the province to its western neighbour, New Brunswick.

Nova Scotia and New Brunswick lie opposite each other across the Bay of Fundy. The Northumberland Strait is to the north, between Nova Scotia and Prince Edward Island. The northern part of Nova Scotia, called Cape Breton Island, is separated from the rest of the province by the Strait of Canso. It can only be reached by a road over a narrow **causeway**. At the northeastern end of Cape Breton Island, the Cabot Strait lies between the province and Newfoundland. Nova Scotia's southeast coast faces out to the Atlantic Ocean.

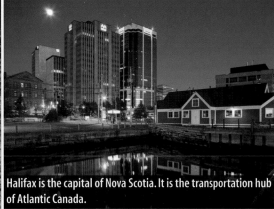

Halifax is the capital of Nova Scotia. It is the transportation hub of Atlantic Canada.

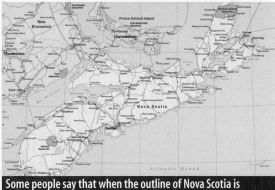

The Bay of Fundy, which lies between Nova Scotia and New Brunswick, has the highest tides on Earth. Twice a day, more than 100 billion tonnes of sea water rush in and out of the bay, often creating a rise and fall of up to about 3.5 metres.

Some people say that when the outline of Nova Scotia is coloured red on a map, it looks like a lobster.

a Scotia has a long and fascinating history. Its past is marked by a ber of battles between France and Britain for control of the region. se battles came to an end when Britain seized France's Fort Louisbourg 758. Fortresses, monuments, old homes and buildings, and many eums around Nova Scotia serve as landmarks to the province's history.

ET FACTS

Most of Nova Scotia's rivers are less than 80 kilometres long. The Mersey and the St. Mary's are the longest rivers in the province.

Drivers can reach Nova Scotia via the Trans-Canada Highway.

The CAT is North America's fastest car ferry. It runs between Bar Harbour and Yarmouth.

There are more than three thousand lakes in Nova Scotia. The largest is the saltwater Bras d'Or Lake.

There are many islands off the Nova Scotia coast. Sable Island is one of the largest.

The Annapolis and Shubenacadie Rivers flow into the Bay of Fundy.

The Fundy tides are so powerful that they sometimes erode the quartz rocks along the shore of Partridge Island.

Halifax has an advantage over American east coast ports because it is always ice-free. It is also a day's sailing time closer to Europe.

ia has a strong heritage. Many the province live shing villages.

LAND AND CLIMATE

Only about 10 percent of the land in Nova Scotia is farmed.

Nova Scotia is made up of rugged highlands, rolling valleys, and a large number of rivers, lakes, and streams. Two kinds of terrain dominate the province. The Atlantic Upland consists of small mountains with thick forests. It covers most of Nova Scotia. Lowlands lie between the uplands. These valley regions are carved out by erosion, caused by wind and water. The major lowland is the Annapolis Valley.

It is wetter and milder along the Nova Scotia coast than it is inland.

The highest temperature in Nova Scotia was recorded at 38.3° Celsius, in 1935. The lowest recorded temperature was −41.1° Celsius, in 1920.

weather in Nova Scotia challenges **meteorologists**. The province between two strong ocean currents: the cold Labrador Current, ch comes from the Arctic Ocean, and the warm Gulf Stream, ch comes from the Gulf of Mexico. The mixing of these two ents results in Nova Scotia's moderate winters and cool mers. It also plays a key role in producing thick sea fogs.

GET FACTS

Halifax has fog at least one day out of every three.

Cape Breton Highlands National Park encompasses 950 square kilometres of beautiful highland and coastal habitats.

Nova Scotia's northern highlands consist of rocks that are about 400 million years old.

The highest point in Nova Scotia is Barren Mountain. It stands 532 metres high.

NATURAL RESOURCES

The soil in Nova Scotia is thin, stony, and not very fertile, except in the Annapolis Valley and along the Northumberland coastal plain.

Water is Nova Scotia's most important resource. The province has many rivers and lakes, which provide Nova Scotians with a huge supply of fresh water, **hydroelectric power**, and transportation routes for the mining and logging industries. The sea provides **ground fish** such as haddock and cod, and shellfish such as scallops and lobsters. Fishing is an essential part of Nova Scotia's economy.

KEEP CONNECTED

Lobsters are abundant in Nova Scotia's waters. They are one of the province's most valuable catches. To learn more about the fishing industry in Nova Scotia, visit **www.mar.dfo-mpo.gc.ca/pande/ecn/ns/e/ns7-e.asp.**

...t discoveries of gas and oil around Sable Island have added to the province's economy.

...t of the province was once covered in forests. Today, forests ...r about 75 percent of the land, but many are secondary growth **...iferous** forests. This means they are made up of new trees that ...e planted to replace ones cut down. Nova Scotia's trees have served ...lumber industry well.

...main mineral resource in Nova Scotia is coal. There are also ...osits of salt and construction minerals such as sand, gypsum, ...gravel in the province.

In May 1992, 26 men were killed in the Westray Mine disaster. In 1998, the remainder of the mine was destroyed.

Pugwash is the site of a large salt mine. Each year, the mine produces more than one million tonnes of the world's purest salt.

PLANTS AND ANIMALS

The fall season brings beautiful colours to Nova Scotia's landscapes.

Blueberries are one of Nova Scotia's most valuable crops.

The northern half of Cape Breton Island is part of the vast coniferous forest that covers most of northern Canada. Trees there include white spruce and balsam fir. To the south, there are mostly spruce, tamarack, hemlock, pine, and fir mixed with some **deciduous** trees such as maple, birch, beech, and ash. Bushes such as clintonia, cranberries, and blueberries can be found in many parts of the province.

Wildflowers such as mayflowers, insect-eating pitcher plants, water lilies, and violets grow throughout the province. Mosses, ferns, and lichens grow in the marshy and rocky areas, and a European import, the cuckooflower, has spread through the Annapolis Valley.

The white-tailed deer is the most common large animal in Nova Scotia.

All kinds of wildlife can be found in Nova Scotia's forests. Large animals such as bears, moose, and deer live there, but smaller animals are more common in the province. Foxes, skunks, porcupines, minks, otters, and weasels are all native to Nova Scotia. Ducks, grouse, pheasants, and bald eagles are among the many birds that frequent the area.

Marine life includes cod, swordfish, trout, lobsters, scallops, and oysters. Whales are a common sight around Digby Neck. Nova Scotia wildlife, like wildlife around the world, is at risk. Since the province burns so much coal to generate electricity, sulphur emissions are a problem. More emissions are carried over the province by westerly winds from the northeastern United States.

The osprey is the provincial bird.

The Nova Scotia duck tolling retriever is the provincial animal.

...ipitation falls through these pollutants and becomes acidic. ...ntually, the lakes become acidic and are unable to support ...life. The Nova Scotia government's main environmental concern ...e improvement of water control and the preservation of salmon ...trout habitats.

GET FACTS

North American porcupines live mostly in coniferous forests.

Nova Scotia's plant life is surprisingly diverse, considering the small size of the province.

The high Fundy tides have created marshy areas that farmers have enclosed with dikes to form farmland.

Every summer, 2 million sand pipers gather on the mud of the Bay of Fundy to feed on mud shrimps before starting their non-stop flight to South America.

There are many provincial parks that are working to preserve Nova Scotia's natural environment. Kejimkujik National Park is perhaps the best known.

The red spruce is Nova Scotia's provincial tree.

Sable Island has the largest breeding colony of grey seals and harbour seals in the western Atlantic.

Nova Scotia's provincial flower is the mayflower.

Thousands of people drive the 43 kilometres from Halifax to see the famous harbour and lighthouse at Peggy's Cove.

Visitors can learn more about Nova Scotia's long and exciting history at many of the province's tourist attractions. Fort Louisbourg on Cape Breton Island was once a seaport and **fortified** town. It was built by the French and destroyed by the British about 250 years ago. The fortress has been rebuilt in accurate detail. Costumed guides in the roles of soldiers, villagers, and noblemen take visitors back to 1744.

The Halifax Citadel National Historic Site is the most visited national site in Canada. Visitors can explore this star-shaped fortress, which was built between 1828 and 1856, and learn more about the naval and military history of Nova Scotia. At the Maritime Museum of the Atlantic, visitors can see exhibits of the Halifax Explosion and artifacts recovered from the *Titanic*, which sank near Halifax in 1912.

The Halifax Citadel National Historic Site features a restored libra detention cells, and barrack rooms from the 1800s.

At the Fortress of Louisbourg National Historic Site, interpreters dress up in period costumes and act out the daily lives of historic townspeople and soldiers.

e than 100,000 visitors a year follow the Evangeline Trail. This goes through the Acadian villages on the Fundy shore to the nstructed Port-Royal National Historic Site, Canada's oldest manent European settlement.

GET FACTS

Alexander Graham Bell, a famous inventor, spent his summers in Baddeck. Today, the Alexander Graham Bell National Historic Site contains a museum honouring his life and work.

The Port Royal Habitation National Historic Site brings visitors back to the early 17th century, when French explorers first settled in Nova Scotia.

Daily re-enactments of 18th-century military life take place at many of Nova Scotia's historical sites.

Nova Scotia has more historic sites than any other province except Quebec.

INDUSTRY

Pictou is one of the largest live lobster harvesting ports in the world.

Service and financial industries are important to Nova Scotia. There are more office buildings, schools, and hotels in the province than there are factories.

Nova Scotia is known for its prominent fishing industry. Cod, haddock, herring, lobster, and scallops are among the fish that contribute to the province's economy.

KEEP CONNECTED

Shipbuilding was an important part of Nova Scotia's history. To learn more about this industry, visit **www.parl.ns.ca/woodenships/why.htm**.

Nova Scotia is an important supplier of Christmas trees. Every year, thousands of evergreens are exported from the province to other markets.

...t of Nova Scotia's farmland is in the Annapolis Valley and in ...hern parts of the province. The province is best known for ...wing fruits and vegetables, but dairy farming is the largest ...cultural sector.

...nufacturing is also an important industry. Iron and steel ...nufacturing, food processing, and paper production are among ...most important manufacturing activities. Most of these ...ll plants process local products such as fish, fruit, livestock, ...pulpwood.

More than two dozen kinds of marine life are harvested in Nova Scotia's waters.

The Annapolis Valley is known for its delicious apple harvests. Most of the apple orchards are family owned.

The first commercial use of Nova Scotia's trees was for shipbuilding.

Nova Scotia is second to British Columbia in the value of its fisheries.

Nova Scotia has about 26,000 kilometres of roadways.

The Halifax harbour is Canada's busiest east coast port. It also serves as Canada's main naval base.

Nova Scotia has an extensive network of roads, railways, and maritime shipping routes. The harbour at Halifax remains ice-free year round and has excellent facilities for ocean-going vessels. It is second only to Montreal in the number of ships that visit. There are more than 750 kilometres of rail lines in the province, many of which are used for shipping goods to other parts of Canada.

Dalhousie University is located in Halifax. It is one of Canada's leading teaching and research universities.

One of Nova Scotia's most important traffic routes is the Canso Causeway. It links mainland Nova Scotia to Cape Breton Island, and it carries both highway and railway traffic. The creation of the causeway made heavy industry possible in Cape Breton. Nova Scotia also has a good roadway system. As the province is so far away from the large markets of central Canada, improvements to the roads are always a priority.

About two-thirds of Nova Scotia's work force are employed in service industries such as transportation, public administration, power generation, finance, retail sales, and health and education. The province has many degree-granting colleges and universities. Dalhousie University is the largest and most well-known of the schools in Nova Scotia.

Highland dancing is taught at the Gaelic College of Celtic Arts and Crafts.

Nova Scotia's main medical research facility is the Faculty of Medicine at Dalhousie University.

...ser known college is the **Gaelic** College of **Celtic** Arts and Crafts. This unique ...ol is located on Cape Breton Island and is dedicated to the preservation of ...c and Gaelic culture in Nova Scotia. It holds courses in the Gaelic language ...offers instruction in such things as Celtic harp, bagpiping, and fiddling.

...o Causeway was ...d in 1955. It ...ars and trains to ...ds to and from ...ton.

The Gaelic College of Celtic Arts and Crafts is the only one of its kind in North America. It is located at St. Ann's Bay, which is the earliest Scottish settlement in Cape Breton.

Canada's first newspaper was the *Halifax Gazette*. It was first published in 1752 but is no longer in circulation.

Service industries are the main economic activity in the province.

The Bank of Nova Scotia is one of the largest banks in Canada.

Sable Island was once called the "Graveyard of the Atlantic." Its shifting sand dunes have been the cause of more than 500 shipwrecks.

Nova Scotia Community College has 18 campuses and learning centres around the province.

The Bedford Institute of Oceanography, in Dartmouth, is one of Canada's largest facilities for conducting research in marine sciences.

About 72 percent of Nova Scotia's electricity is produced by coal-burning power stations, and 13 percent is produced by oil. The rest comes from tidal power on the Annapolis River.

The Mi'kmaq's traditional way of life changed drastically when large numbers of settlers moved into Nova Scotia and onto their land.

For centuries before European explorers arrived, thousands of Mi'kmaq lived in the Nova Scotia region. The first Europeans they met were probably Vikings. The waters and woods in the Nova Scotia region were rich in fish and wildlife, and the Mi'kmaq lived mostly by hunting and fishing. They would live near the seashore in the summer, where they could easily catch fish. In the winter, they would move into the woods where they would hunt for wildlife and take shelter from the cold.

KEEP CONNECTED

The Nova Scotia Museum has more than 700 portraits and illustrations showing the traditional Mi'kmaq ways of life. To view these images online, visit **http://museum.gov. ns.ca/mikmaq**.

The Mi'kmaq developed a canoe made out of a white cedar frame, covered in white birchbark, which could carry up to 1,800 kilograms.

Mi'kmaq were skilled at fishing and hunting. Fishing was often
at night from canoes. The Mi'kmaq carried birchbark torches
speared the fish that were attracted by the light. They also used
rches to surprise and attract birds. Hunting large animals was
ved for the winter, when snow made it harder for the animals
cape.

In the early 1500s, the Mi'kmaq traded goods with European fishers who came to Canada every year. Furs would be traded for goods such as guns and beads.

Nova Scotia place names such as Musquodoboit, Shubenacadie, and Pugwash come from the Mi'kmaq language.

The Mi'kmaq had many legends about a spirit called Glooscap, who was responsible for shaping much of the landscape.

EXPLORERS

Viking explorers may have reached Nova Scotia about five centuries before John Cabot arrived on Cape Breton Island in 1497. Cabot claimed the Nova Scotia region for Henry VII of England, then left. Tales that fish could be scooped from the sea in baskets soon brought European fishing boats to the northeast coast. Explorers also came.

Jacques Cartier passed through the Cabot Strait in 1534 and claimed the land he saw for King Francis I of France. It was not until 1605 that Europeans truly began to settle in Nova Scotia. That year, French explorers Pierre de Monts and Samuel de Champlain, along with 125 colonists, arrived on St. Croix Island, which is between New Brunswick and Maine.

The people at Port Royal founded the "Order of Good Cheer," which was dedicated to making evening's meal a happy and memorable event

The next spring, they set up a permanent farming settlement at Port Royal, located on the southwest coast of what is now Nova Scotia. The French named the whole Maritime region Acadia, which was a mythical name meaning "peaceful land."

In 1906, artist Ernest Board painted *Cabot Leaves the Port of Bristol*. The painting is an imaginary scene depicting how the atmosphere may have appeared when Cabot set sail from Great Britain in 1497.

...ctual spot of John Cabot's 1497 landing is questionable—he and his crew landed either in Labrador, Newfoundland, or on Cape Breton.

GET FACTS

A stone with **runic** writing on it was found in 1812 near Yarmouth. The fact that the Vikings used this form of writing suggests that they may have explored the area long ago.

Although both Britain and France claimed the land in the Nova Scotia region, neither nation was interested in settlement. The English were interested in the fur trade and the French in the fisheries.

Port Royal was abandoned after two years, re-established in 1610, then destroyed three years later by an English pirate.

EARLY SETTLERS

An American poet named Henry Wadsworth Longfellow made Nova Scotia famous in his poem "Evangeline." The poem tells how Acadians were driven from their homes in Nova Scotia by British troops. Today, an area of the province is nicknamed "Land of Evangeline."

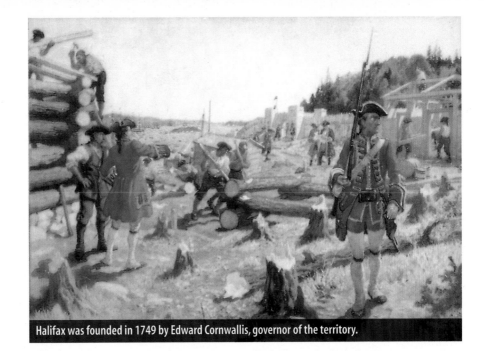

Halifax was founded in 1749 by Edward Cornwallis, governor of the territory.

Over the next century, there were many battles and disputes between the British and the French over ownership of the Maritime region. In 1713, an agreement called the Treaty of Utrecht gave all of Acadia, except Cape Breton Island and Prince Edward Island, to Britain. The British allowed the Acadians to stay as long as they promised loyalty to Britain. The Acadians refused, but promised instead to remain **neutral** in any struggles between France and Britain.

The British settlement of Nova Scotia began with the founding of Halifax in 1749. Thousands of settlers came from Britain and other parts of Europe, and many more arrived from the British colonies in America. As conflicts with France continued, the British were concerned that the Acadians would side with the French. In an effort to prevent this possibility, the British **expelled** more than 6,000 Acadians and moved them to other colonies in 1755.

Nova Scotia's population continued to increase. Britain offered free land to potential settlers in order to attract people to the region. More immigrants from Scotland, Ireland, and England arrived, along with New Englanders. In 1763, the French, through the Treaty of Paris, gave their lands in North America to the British. At this time, many of the deported Acadians returned to the Maritimes and built new settlements.

Loyalists were colonists who remained loyal to Britain during the American Revolution.

During the American Revolution (1775-1783), about 30,000 Loyalists immigrated to the Nova Scotia region. These people were colonists who wished to remain loyal to Britain, and therefore did not want to stay in the newly independent United States. A large amount of building took place with the many new settlers who came to make their homes in the region. By the mid 1800s, construction of military bases, mining, and farming were all well underway in Nova Scotia.

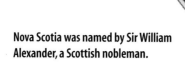

Nova Scotia was named by Sir William Alexander, a Scottish nobleman.

arrival of the Loyalists doubled the population of Nova Scotia in just one year. The population grew so large with the arrival of the Loyalists it had to be divided into smaller colonies.

Many Acadians escaped deportation. Those who avoided deportation were in danger of being killed if they were caught.

The 1758 fall of Louisbourg, which was built to protect the French fishing interests, marked the end of the French colonies in Canada.

American settlers introduced the importance of town meetings and elections to Nova Scotians.

In 1784, Nova Scotia, New Brunswick, and Cape Breton Island were made into separate colonies. Cape Breton Island was reunited with Nova Scotia in 1820.

Between 1815 and 1838, about 20,000 Scottish people and many Irish people came to Canada. A large number chose Nova Scotia as their home.

The ferry between Dartmouth and Halifax is a popular way to commute between the cities.

here are just under one million people living in Nova Scotia. The population is distributed quite evenly throughout the province. The Halifax [Reg]ional Municipality is the financial, cultural, and [com]mercial centre of Nova Scotia. With about 359,111 [inh]abitants, it makes up more than one third of the [pro]vincial population.

[Nea]rly 147,454 people live in the second-biggest [com]munity, the Cape Breton Regional Municipality, [whi]ch includes Sydney and Louisbourg. Although always [a fi]shing and fish processing area, it is now developing [info]rmation technology, machinery, and ocean sciences.

There are said to be more Scottish clans in Nova Scotia than in Scotland, and some Nova Scotians of Scottish descent still speak Gaelic.

[No]va Scotia's heartland community is the [tow]n of Truro, which has been an [agr]icultural marketplace for [gen]erations. Yarmouth has strong [con]nections with the New [Eng]land states across the Bay [of F]undy because of its [com]mon history of fishing [and] commerce.

Halifax is the biggest city in the Maritimes.

Dartmouth and Halifax are often called twin cities. Dartmouth is situated northeast of Halifax, across the harbour.

People of British descent make up about 80 percent of Nova Scotia's population.

In 1996, the cities of Halifax and Dartmouth, along with the rest of Halifax County, were combined to form the Halifax Regional Municipality.

There are about 7,770 Mi'kmaq in Nova Scotia.

Acadians make up about 12 percent of Nova Scotia's population.

About 93 percent of Nova Scotians speak English as their first language.

POLITICS AND GOVERNMENT

Nova Scotia's Legislative Assembly meets at Province House in downtown Halifax. Province House is Canada's oldest Parliament building.

Nova Scotia was among the first Canadian provinces. In 1867, Nova Scotia, New Brunswick, Quebec, and Ontario formed the Dominion of Canada. The province is governed by a one-chamber legislature, with 52 members. The majority party forms the government, and its leader is the premier, who appoints a cabinet. The cabinet sets government policy, and each minister is responsible for seeing that his or her department carries out these policies.

Below the provincial legislature is the regional, city, town, or rural municipality. The municipal government is responsible for local services but, in the last 30 or 40 years, the province has taken over many of these.

Women in Nova Scotia received the right to vote on April 26, 1918.

Nova Scotia is represented federally by 11 members in the House of Commons and nine Senators.

Scotia has always had problems with raising money
se it is small and not heavily industrialized. It also has
h unemployment rate and must often turn to the federal
rnment for help. Despite economic problems, Nova
ans remain hopeful and determined to build a more
perous province.

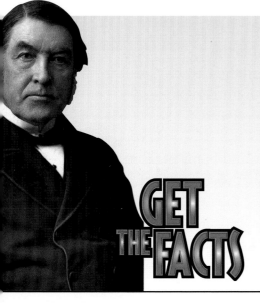

Sir Charles Tupper was one of three prime ministers of Canada that came from Nova Scotia. The others were Sir John Sparrow, David Thompson, and Sir Robert Laird Borden.

Nova Scotia's provincial motto is *Munit haec et altera vincit*, which means "One defends and the other conquers."

The provincial government employs large numbers of people in its Halifax departments and its regional offices.

In the late 1800s, many Nova Scotians wanted to withdraw from **Confederation**. On the anniversary of Confederation, they would hang black crepe on their buildings to show they were in mourning.

CULTURAL GROUPS

Nova Scotians of Scottish descent celebrate their heritage with customs such as bagpiping and Highland dancing.

Perhaps the strongest cultural presence in Nova Scotia is the Scottish. People of Scottish descent make up about 25 percent of the province's population. Festivals that celebrate Scottish heritage are held throughout Nova Scotia. The Antigonish Highland Games are among the province's most famous Scottish celebrations. Held every July since 1863, the Highland Games are an excellent demonstration of art, strength, and skill. Athletic competitions, Highland dancing, pipe band competitions, and art displays are all part of the games. Other Scottish festivals include the International Gathering of the Clans in Halifax and the Celtic Colours International Festival, where the sounds of fiddles, pipes, and singing can be heard all over Cape Breton.

Acadians live mostly in northeastern Cape Breton, and many of them continue to speak the Acadian **dialect** of French that was developed long ago. The Acadians in Nova Scotia are proud of their culture, and they share their pride with others through various festivals and fairs. The Grand-Pré National Historic Site was established as a memory to the Acadian settlers who were deported to British colonies. A stone

Lunenburg hosts Oktoberfest celebrations every year.

Planked salmon is a distinct Nova Scotian dish. Other well-known dishes include Acadian rappie pie, Lunenburg pudding, tangy Solomon Gundy, and blueberry grunt.

rch on the site serves as a museum that exhibits Acadian history. , the Acadian Museum, in the town of Chéticamp, features ich-Canadian antiques, glassware, and rugs.

re is still a relatively large population of Mi'kmaq in Nova ia. Most Mi'kmaq live on one of the 13 reserves in the province, many others have moved into towns and cities. The Mi'kmaq brate their distinct culture at Chapel Island Mission and the burne County Museum, which displays artifacts detailing the 's Mi'kmaq history.

West Pubnico holds an Acadian festival every summer. One of the most popular features of the festival is the children's parade.

Nova Scotia celebrates African Heritage Month every February.

Street signs in the town of Pugwash are in both Gaelic and English.

Dutch, Hungarians, and Italians make up small minorities in Nova Scotia.

The Black Cultural Centre for Nova Scotia, near Dartmouth, celebrates Nova Scotia's African-Canadian heritage with exhibits and special events.

ARTS AND ENTERTAINMENT

Sarah McLachlan studied classical guitar, piano, and voice while growing up in Halifax.

Nova Scotia has a rich tradition of music that ranges from Acadian jigs to Celtic rock. Towns and villages throughout the province are filled with song year round. Bagpiping and fiddling contests are a major part of the Antigonish Highland Games. They can also be heard at the Gaelic Mod at St. Ann's and at the International Gathering of the Clans in Halifax. Many Nova Scotian musicians are appreciated around the world. Anne Murray, from Springhill, has sold more than 20 million albums. Sarah McLachlan, originally from Halifax, has released several top-selling albums.

There is more to Nova Scotia's arts scene than great music. The province is home to many excellent theatre companies and programs. Festival Antigonish is a summer theatre celebration. Drama, musicals, comedies, and children's plays are performed throughout July and August. The Neptune Theatre in Halifax presents many lively plays throughout the year.

Three Black Cats is just one example of Maud Lewis' cheerful paintings. Thousands of people from Canada and the rest of the world visit the galleries that display her colourful work.

Every September, Mahone Bay holds the Great Scarecrow Festival and Antique Fair. Scarecrows, square dancing, musicals, fiddling, and craft demonstrations are all part of the fun.

that celebrates Maritime culture can be found all over the The Art Gallery of Nova Scotia in Halifax displays works of artists, as well as paintings from around the world. Folk art throughout the province, especially at Scottish festivals Craft festivals attract many visitors every year.

Folk
ery July
es top
all over

The Nova Scotia Mass Choir is a talented, energetic gospel choir based in Halifax. Their music has been so well received that they now have a CD and a television series.

In August, jugglers, musicians, magicians, acrobats, and actors show off their talents at The Halifax International Busker Festival.

Maud Lewis is known as the mother of Nova Scotian folk art.

The Men of the Deeps are a group of miners or ex-miners who have sung all over the world of their hard life working below the ground.

The Atlantic Jazz Festival is held in Halifax every July.

The Rankin Family is a North American band from Nova Scotia. Other well-known Nova Scotian performers include the Barra MacNeils, Natalie MacMaster, and Rita MacNeil.

The Chester Playhouse presents concerts, comedies, and dramas to Chester residents and visitors.

Rafters on the Shubenacadie River will experience the power of the Bay of Fundy tides.

In 1946, the original *Bluenose* ran aground on a coral reef and sank. The *Bluenose II* was built in 1963 and is an exact replica of the earlier ship. It is berthed at Halifax and also sails out of Lunenburg.

Nova Scotia's seafaring tradition is still alive in the many residents who sail and windsurf, especially in the warmer waters of the Northumberland Strait. The *Bluenose*, a famous Nova Scotian **schooner**, was victorious many times during the 1920s and 1930s in the International Fisherman's Trophy races.

Rafting is another popular water sport in Nova Scotia. The powerful Fundy tides push against the flow of the river and create waves, called **tidal bores**, that move upstream. Rafting on tidal bores is an exciting summertime activity.

Nova Scotia has many beautiful beaches that attract visitors from around Canada and the rest of the world.

With a quarter of the population being of Scottish descent, Highland games competitions are popular. The games have athletes running a 8-kilometre road race, throwing a hammer, and tossing the caber. A caber is a peeled log, about 8 metres long and 15 centimetres in diameter, the size of a small telephone pole. Athletes must hold the caber upright in their hands and lean it against their shoulders. Then, they must toss it end over end. The toss requires immense skill and strength.

In the hammer throw, athletes throw a Scottish hammer, which consists of a 7-kilogram metal ball with a wooden handle attached to it. The athlete must not move his or her feet when the hammer is thrown. The stone throw is another event. The athlete must throw an 11-kilogram rock, shot-put style, with only one hand. Each contestant gets three throws, but only the longest throw is counted in final scoring.

The Antigonish Highland Games are the longest running Highland games in North America. They have been held since 1863.

Experts rate the golf courses of Nova Scotia among the best in the country.

...s commonly thought that hockey was invented by English soldiers ...o were stationed in Halifax. Stick and ball games were popular in ...gland, and soldiers found these games easy to adapt to Nova ...tia's winter conditions. Later, a puck took the place of the ball ...ause it was easier to control. Several Nova Scotian players, ...luding Sidney Crosby, play in the National Hockey League. ...athan Sim and Colin White, who played together as juniors in ...w Glasgow, opposed each other in the 1999 Stanley Cup finals. ...wmobiling, cross-country skiing, and curling are favourite ...ter sports.

GET THE FACTS

Bluenose has been on every Canadian dime since 1937.

The National Universities Basketball Championships are played annually at the Metro Centre in Halifax.

Teams of military personnel from all over the world compete in gun running, hurdles, obstacle courses, and pipe and brass band competitions at the Royal Nova Scotia International Tattoo.

CANADA

Canada is a vast nation, and each province and territory has its own unique features. This map shows important information about each of Canada's 10 provinces and three territories, including when they joined Confederation, their size, population, and capital city. For more information about Canada, visit **http://canada.gc.ca**.

Alberta
Entered Confederation: 1905
Capital: Edmonton
Area: 661,848 sq km
Population: 3,632,483

British Columbia
Entered Confederation: 1871
Capital: Victoria
Area: 944,735 sq km
Population: 4,419,974

Manitoba
Entered Confederation: 1870
Capital: Winnipeg
Area: 647,797 sq km
Population: 1,213,815

New Brunswick
Entered Confederation: 1867
Capital: Fredericton
Area: 72,908 sq km
Population: 748,319

Newfoundland and Labrador
Entered Confederation: 1949
Capital: St. John's
Area: 405,212 sq km
Population: 508,990

SYMBOLS OF NOVA SCOTIA

FLAG

COAT OF ARMS

TREE
Red Spruce

Map Labels

0   200   400 Kilometers
0   200   400 Miles

Baffin Bay

Baffin Island

Davis Strait

Iqaluit (Frobisher Bay)

Ivujivik

Labrador Sea

NEWFOUNDLAND

Schefferville

Happy Valley-Goose Bay

Island of Newfoundland

Chisasibi (Fort George)

Gander

Saint John's

QUEBEC

Sept-Iles

Gulf of St. Lawrence

St. Pierre and Miquelon (FRANCE)

onee

Chibougamau

PRINCE EDWARD ISLAND

Sydney

NEW BRUNSWICK

Charlottetown

Fredericton

Quebec

Saint John

Halifax

Sherbrooke

Montreal

NOVA SCOTIA

udbury

Ottawa

Lake Ontario

Toronto

Hamilton

London

Lake Erie

BIRD
Osprey

FRUIT
Wild Blueberry

ANIMAL
Duck Tolling Retriever

Northwest Territories
Entered Confederation: 1870
Capital: Yellowknife
Area: 1,346,106 sq km
Population: 42,940

Nova Scotia
Entered Confederation: 1867
Capital: Halifax
Area: 55,284 sq km
Population: 939,531

Nunavut
Entered Confederation: 1999
Capital: Iqaluit
Area: 2,093,190 sq km
Population: 531,556

Ontario
Entered Confederation: 1867
Capital: Toronto
Area: 1,076,395 sq km
Population: 12,986,857

Prince Edward Island
Entered Confederation: 1873
Capital: Charlottetown
Area: 5,660 sq km
Population: 140,402

Quebec
Entered Confederation: 1867
Capital: Quebec City
Area: 1,542,056 sq km
Population: 7,782,561

Saskatchewan
Entered Confederation: 1905
Capital: Regina
Area: 651,036 sq km
Population: 1,023,810

Yukon
Entered Confederation: 1898
Capital: Whitehorse
Area: 482,443 sq km
Population: 33,442

BRAIN TEASERS

Test your knowledge of Nova Scotia by trying to answer these mind-boggling brain teaser

1 Multiple Choice

Nova Scotia is the _____ smallest province in Canada.
a) tenth
b) fifth
c) second
d) ninth

2 True or False?

People of British descent make up about 80 percent of Nova Scotia's population.

3 Multiple Choice

What is the capital of Nova Scotia?
a) Chester
b) Halifax
c) Wolfville
d) Cape Breton

4 Multiple Choice

Which European expl were first to explore Nova Scotia?
a) Vikings
b) British
c) French
d) Germans

5 Multiple Choice

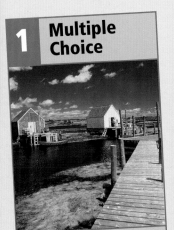

Some people say that when the outline of Nova Scotia is coloured red on a map it looks like this animal.
a) lobster
b) bear
c) snake
d) deer

6 True or False?

It is commonly thought that hockey was invented by the Mi'kmaq.

7 Multiple Choice

What is Nova Scotia's most important resource?
a) oil
b) wheat
c) lumber
d) water

8 Multiple Choice

Nova Scotia is best kn for growing what?
a) wheat
b) fruits and vegetab
c) canola
d) tobacco

va Scotia is the second smallest province in Canada.   2. True   3. B, Halifax is the capital of Nova Scotia.   4. A, The Vikings were the first European rs to explore Nova Scotia.   5. A, When the the outline of Nova Scotia is coloured red on a map, it looks like a lobster.   6. False, It is commonly thought that soldiers stationed in Halifax invented hockey.   7. Water is Nova Scotia's most important resource.   8. B, Nova Scotia is best known for growing fruits etables.